MW00990208

Living
Check to
MONDAY

The Real Deal About Money, Credit and Financial Security

Living
Check to
MONDAY

The Real Deal About Money,
Credit and Financial Security

By Lynn Richardson
"The Mortgage Guru"

Lynn Richardson Enterprises, Inc.
PO Box 2815
Country Club Hills, IL 60478
Phone: (888) LYN.N123 - (888.596.6123)
Email: dreamscometrue@lynnrichardson.com
Website: www.lynnrichardson.com

ISBN 10: 0-9773232-0-X
ISBN 13: 978-0-9773232-0-3

Cover Designed by: 1st Choice Publications

To every person who is in debt,

To all people who live beyond their means,

To every person who prayed for a book about money that deals with regular, everyday issues in regular, everyday language . . .

This book is for regular people.

Acknowledgments

*F*irst, I must say thank you to the true Author of this book, the One I serve, and the Source through which all blessings flow . . . God. Most of what is shared in this work is from personal life experience, and I truly thank God for blessing me with the tests to share this testimony.

I thank my husband, Demietrius, and my daughters, Cydney, Taylor, and Kennedy, for their love and support and for being the inspiration for my earthly aspirations.

I thank Grandma Bea, who raised me, and who showed me undying love and support from infancy and who always made me feel as if I could conquer the world.

I thank my parents who passed on the gift of gab and curiosity (mom) and the gift of discernment and strategy (dad) that have contributed to my success.

I thank my aunt, Josylyn Adams, my second "mom", Diane Holda, and my sisters in Christ, Marva Nicholson, Shan Wright and Marla Marshall, for being positive forces of hope that have transformed my life.

I thank my Soror, friend, sister and Counselor, Deadra Woods Stokes, for "pulling my coat-tail" and for seeing the bigger picture when I needed you most and I thank my Soror, mentor, and friend,

Lori Jones Gibbs (The Legend), for allowing God to use you to transform the way the world sees wealth.

I thank Melody Spann Cooper and Latrice Spann Levitt for hearing my radio voice before I knew it even existed.

I thank my business partners, colleagues, Sorors, friends, and spiritual advisors for all of your kind words, thoughts, prayers and support.

Table of Contents

Foreword

*T*his little, yet powerful "how to guide" was written with clarity and simplicity to teach you the rules of the money game. It's a practical approach that will give you the wisdom and skills to protect your resources and transform your financial future.

The news is constantly reporting foreclosures, bankruptcies, and job losses at a rate unlike ever before.

Lynn Richardson, passionate media expert and dynamic speaker, is on a mission to educate people on how to rescue themselves from financial disasters. Known as "The Mortgage Guru," Lynn, through her radio program, has helped thousands of people get a new beginning, create wealth, and reclaim control of their lives. Because of Lynn's practical principles, people can relate to Lynn, who is committed to providing hope and methods of financial empowerment that enable them to get back on top again.

Living Check to Monday (CTM), by Lynn, is a tool that provides people with "common sense" although not commonly practiced strategies that will lead them out of debt and provide a path to financial recovery.

Living Check to Monday is a practical book because it is written in everyday language so everyone can understand "the real deal about money, credit and financial security."

With passion and unstoppable drive, Lynn inspires and encourages people not to allow their circumstances to dictate their future. She has been recognized nationally as one of the top performers in the mortgage industry, and as a master workshop presenter and electrifying speaker.

It has been said that most people fail in life because "they don't know that they don't know and they THINK they know." Lynn is providing you with the key to unlock the door to financial bondage.

Read and free yourself!

Les Brown, author of:
Live Your Dreams
It's Not Over Until You Win
Up Thoughts for Down Times

Introduction

"*T*he lack of money is the root of all evil." That's it. I saw that profound imprint on a t-shirt once and said to myself, "that's it." Millions of Americans do not enjoy the benefits of living in a free society because of poor credit, no savings plan, limited financial resources, and the Check-to-Monday syndrome. The common phrase "living from check-to-check" implies that one has enough money to last until the next pay period. Wouldn't it be great if we all had enough money to last from one pay period to the next? Wouldn't it be easier to face each day if we got paid on Friday, the 1st, paid all of the current bills on time, bought groceries, paid for childcare, and had enough money — for transportation, gas, moderate entertainment, and minor emergencies — to last until the next payday, two Fridays away, on the 15th?

That's living from check-to-check. That's how most of us define our current money dilemma, right? Wrong!

The fact is this: most poor and middle class people are living from Check-to-Monday. We'll call it the CTM Syndrome. This is a whole 'nother game. The real deal is this: when most of us get paid on Friday, the 1st, we pay the minimum amount on <u>past due bills</u>, we buy enough groceries to make it through the next seven to ten days, we negotiate the minimum payment with the major utility companies to "keep the lights on", we splurge on a few weekend luxuries like pizza and movies because "we deserve to have *some* fun, don't we?", we put the current bills on the back burner until next month, and by Monday, the 4th, we are essentially broke, right? Right! The 15th, which is a menacing 11 days away, may as well be next year!

The CTM syndrome is even more desperate for those of us who get paid once per month. Whew!

And by the way, if you think you got it goin' on because you got a job making $60,000 a year, you live in a nice neighborhood, but you are the main one in line for a prescription to cure your case of the CTM Syndrome, guess what!

You're poor!

So don't be fooled, keep on reading and tell all of your friends, because help is on the way.

So what do we do about this CTM Syndrome? What have you done about it? Are you living in this stressful situation with no thought as to how you will break free from these invisible money-cuffs? Are your nights sleepless and your days blurred because the creditors are calling you and you can't even figure out how you're going to buy food to eat? Are you near a mental breakdown because you are working two jobs to make the ends meet, or even worse, you're working one job and living with a partner who won't work at all? Are you paving your path to prison, in trouble right now, or already locked up because you said *"Forget it! I'm about to get my hustle on!"* but you got caught?

Whatever the case, we need to find out where your case of the CTM Syndrome began. Does one or more of the following scenarios describe your birth into the CTM Syndrome?

Keeping up with the Jones's
Did you finally get a job making a decent salary, find yourself a nice apartment to rent, furnish it to the max, buy a brand-new vehicle, update your already closet-filled wardrobe weekly (even though you already had clothes with the tags still on), all to impress your "friends", but find yourself with no savings, no "just in case" money, and not even one asset that will increase in value over time?

The credit trap resulting from trying to keep up with the Jones's
Better yet, did you respond to the first 15 credit card offers you got after high school graduation, charge them up to the max, and then discover you didn't have enough money to pay the monthly bills, so before you even stepped one foot into the real world, your credit was ruined?

Money suicide resulting from having only one stream of income
Are you legitimately in money-cuffs because you got laid off or downsized and you can't find a comparable job to pay you *at least* what you were making before "the man" did you in?

Parenthood to young
Did you have a child before you got out of high school, without the knowledge that teenage parenthood makes it more than 95% likely that you would live a life of poverty?

Spending Addiction
Do you walk into your local discount stores with the intention of buying toothpaste and toilet tissue, but walk out with one hundred seventy-nine dollars and forty-seven cents worth of stuff you don't really need?

The Solution
Everything that has a beginning has an ending. Whatever the cause of your case of the CTM Syndrome, understand that money is a game, there are rules, and you must master the rules of this game in order to win the money race. The distance between the beginning point and the ending point depends on you.

I know, you are tired of all the books about money that don't apply to the real life situations of poor people who were born poor and whose mommas and daddies were born poor.

You're tired of the so-called "money gurus" you hear giving solutions to so called problems you **wish** you had! ("How to increase the return on your stock in half the time" — I know, you wish you *had* some stock to even consider increasing!) I feel your pain, so we all have been rescued. This book will guide you through the practical steps necessary to permanently eliminate the symptoms and conditions of the CTM Syndrome.

You picked up this book, borrowed it from a friend, bought it out of desperation, or whatever. The point is, you have it now, so consider yourself equipped with the rules of the money game and the Bylaws of your very own business called "**Me, Inc.**"

Pay <u>Me, Inc.</u> First

Y ou've always dreamed of owning your own business. Why didn't God give you Oprah's talent? Why didn't he bless you with the vision of a computer conglomerate called Microsoft? Well guess what, you already own a business called **Me, Inc.**, and **Me, Inc.** can be a powerful conglomerate or a struggling little shop. It's entirely up to you, I mean, **Me, Inc.**

Every business provides some type of good or some kind of service in exchange for what we know today as money. Businesses that provide goods get the materials for those goods and then sell the finished product to people like you and me in order to make a profit. Your favorite hamburger chain, let's call it **Burger, Inc.**, doesn't have a cow farm in the backyard. **Burger, Inc.** gets beef from **Beef, Inc.** in exchange for money, and then **Burger, Inc.** sells its double cheeseburgers to people like you and me in exchange for more money than it gave **Beef, Inc.** This is called the initial profit.

With the initial profit, **Burger, Inc.** pays its "bills" in this order:

1. **Burger, Inc. (the owner)** — this money is used to duplicate **Burger, Inc.** **Burger, Inc.** duplicates itself by building another **Burger, Inc.** (franchising), buying more commercials to attract more customers to sell more

burgers, and purchasing larger orders of beef to make more burgers to sell to more customers.

2. **Everybody else** — this money is used to pay **Burger, Inc.**'s necessities and bills, like employees, franchise fees, creditors, utilities, legal fees, and employee medical benefits.

3. **Shareholders** — this money, called dividends, is shared with shareholders (investors) who helped **Burger, Inc.** get on its feet, or will help **Burger, Inc.** buy new feet at some time in the future. These shareholders (investors) continue to give **Burger, Inc.** more money (buying more stock in **Burger, Inc.**) because **Burger, Inc.** makes the investors even more dividends than the investors gave **Burger, Inc.** in the first place!

Read number three again, so it can sink in.

And the cycle continues.

If **Burger, Inc.** doesn't have enough money for "**Everybody Else**", then **Burger Inc.** cuts its expenses (people get laid off) or sells more burgers. It's that simple.

That's how **Burger Inc.** stays in business. **Burger, Inc.** won't be in business if the owner of **Burger, Inc.** doesn't duplicate itself and generate enough money to satisfy the basic needs required to keep up with the competition to make the burgers better, faster, and/or tastier. **Burger, Inc.** won't be in business if it doesn't develop a plan to cut its expenses or increase the number of burgers it sells when times get rough.

Do you see the similarities and differences between **Burger, Inc.** and **Me, Inc.**? Remember, all businesses provide either goods or services in exchange for money. **Burger, Inc.** provides goods, i.e, burgers, in exchange for money. **Me, Inc.** provides services every day, and sometimes goods too! For now, I will deal with services and we will discuss goods later, in Bylaw Six.

Me, Inc. starts each day clothing and feeding people and continues each workday providing services to places like **Job, Inc.** in exchange for money. I bet you're thinking, *"Okay, Miss Smarty Pants, I'm losing the money game before it starts, because with all of my bills, **Me, Inc.** doesn't have an initial profit."* Right? Wrong, again! **Me, Inc.** does indeed have an initial profit, every month, or every two weeks, or every week, or whenever **Me, Inc.** receives a paycheck for the services it provided to **Job, Inc.**

With it's initial profit, or paycheck, however, **Me, Inc.** pays its bills in this order:

1. **Everybody else** — this money is used to pay **Me, Inc.**'s necessities and bills, like child care providers, rent, utilities, gas, car notes, and even some of the things **Me, Inc.** really doesn't need like weekly hairdo's, too many café whatevers, and the latest designer clothing.

2. **Me, Inc.** (the owner) — the owner never gets paid because there is no money left after **Everybody Else** is paid.

3. **Share Holders** — forget it, there is definitely no money to "share" with shareholders and because of this, no one will invest in you, I mean **Me, Inc.** Neither banks, nor

mortgage companies, nor finance companies, will give you a penny because you won't invest in yourself a mere tenth of what you want other people to invest in you!

Oops, did I say *"you"*? Sorry, I meant **Me, Inc.**

I know you see the similarities between **Burger, Inc.** and **Me, Inc.** The major difference between **Burger, Inc.** and **Me, Inc.**, however, is that **Me, Inc.** never sees a net profit because **Me, Inc.** dispenses its initial profit in the wrong order! So, guess what? **Me, Inc.** cannot and should not attempt to duplicate itself. Because **Me, Inc.** cannot duplicate it self, **Me, Inc.** will never get bigger or better or live beyond one life cycle or generation. If the world was full of these kinds of **Me, Inc.**s, the human race would have been extinct long ago.

But you're hard-headed.

Me, Inc. decides to duplicate itself anyway, by franchising prematurely (bringing children into the world before you are financially mature), so **Me, Inc.** has increased its expenses without increasing its initial profit and guess what, **Me, Inc.** either gets desperate and goes out of business (files bankruptcy, picks up an illegal money-making hobby, or literally goes crazy), or barely stays in business.

And barely staying in business means the CTM Syndrome begins.

In either case, **Me, Inc.** is through and so are you.

So, the moral of the story is this: **YOU MUST PAY ME, INC. FIRST!**

How much?

Ten percent of your initial profit. That's it. Pay **Me, Inc.** the first ten percent of everything you bring in. Your paycheck — pay **Me, Inc.** ten percent. The money you collected for doing your auntie's bridesmaids' hair for the wedding — pay **Me, Inc.** ten percent. Your social security check — pay **Me, Inc.** ten percent. Your baby's daddy's child support payment if you're lucky or the random donation if you're not — whatever it is and however frequent, pay **Me, Inc.** ten percent. You get the point.

Now, I know what you're thinking. *"Okay Miss Smarty Pants. I will never have enough to pay **Me, Inc.** first because I already don't have enough money to pay **Everybody Else."*** Right? You are wrong, again. Let me break it down for you.

Let's say your initial profit, your paycheck, is $1,000. Then what I'm asking you to do, no, excuse me, what the rules of the money game demand, is that you pay **Me, Inc.** the first ten percent, or $100. **Everybody Else** still has $900 — not bad, since **Everybody Else** did absolutely nothing to help **Me, Inc.** get the initial profit in the first place!

So the initial profit is $1,000 and **Me, Inc.** gets the first ten percent — a cool one hundred dollars. You may think $100 really isn't a lot of money, but its consistency guarantees that **Me, Inc.** can one day duplicate itself.

And besides, **Everybody Else** still has $900 left to work with.

Even if your lights are about to be turned off, the fact of the matter is this: *Whatever hole your financial situation has gotten you into, the $100 that you need to save for **Me, Inc.** is hardly the* *determining factor in getting you out.* Since the $100 really can't break you, then choose to let it make you.

Pay **Me, Inc.** first.

Always.

Pay Me, Inc. First Daily Principles

1. **Me, Inc.** will be just like **Burger, Inc.**

2. **Me, Inc.** will keep the first 10% of every dollar **Me, Inc.** receives.

3. **Me, Inc.** will store the first 10% of every dollar it receives in a savings account in a small bank, credit union, or savings and loan on the other side of town.

4. **Me, Inc.** will not receive a cash station card, debit card, or any other kind of card for this savings account.

5. **Me, Inc.** will teach **Son, Inc.** and **Daughter, Inc.** to keep the first 10% of every dollar they earn as well.

6. **Me, Inc.** will not get nervous if the lights are going to be cut off – no matter what, **Me, Inc.** will keep the first 10%.

7. **Me, Inc.** will pay **Everybody Else** with the remaining 90% of its initial profit.

Bylaw Number Two:
Schedule Your Money

I know you're still not quite over **Bylaw Number One** and I know you are having some trouble. I know what you're thinking. *"Okay Miss Smarty Pants. So what if I do pay **Me, Inc.** the first ten percent of my initial profit? I was in the hole before and I didn't have enough money to pay **Everybody Else** then, and now I am really screwed, because my lights will be cut off or my rent won't get paid."* Right?

Wrong!

Remember what **Burger, Inc.** did. When times got tough, **Burger, Inc.** sold more burgers or it cut its expenses. We'll deal with "selling more burgers" in **Bylaw Number Six**. Right now, we're going to cut expenses. **Burger, Inc.** fired some folk and **Me, Inc.** needs to ditto that.

Oh yeah, you have some people on your payroll, whether you know it or not. The lady who does the same toes you can polish your own self — give her a pink slip. The guy who details the same car you can wash with your own soap and water (and get some much needed exercise too!) — PINK SLIP! Now, don't play me, you know what a pink slip is!

The babysitter who doesn't even watch the kids while you go to the club — double pink slip for the babysitter <u>and</u> the club.

The expensive coffee shop that serves the same thing you can make with some French Vanilla creamer, a touch of whipped cream and a couple packets of sugar — pink slip.

The point is this — you need to get unproductive **Employees** and unnecessary **Expenses** off of **Me, Inc.**'s payroll!

But before we start cutting folks, we need to know who **Employees** and **Expenses** are. So, on behalf of **Me, Inc.**, you need to "Schedule your Money." I didn't say budget, because I knew you would have issues with that word. So, let's say "schedule" your money. In order to schedule anything, you have to know (1) what is being scheduled and (2) when it is going to take place. It also helps that if you have two or more events taking place at any given time, that you write those things down so you won't double book your events or forget one of them.

When you begin to schedule your money, you will be amazed by the number of groupies who had been hanging around **Me, Inc.** and who had been soaking up **Me, Inc.**'s attention *and* money.

When you begin to schedule your money, you will notice how your "friends" won't be so quick to order those drinks you used to pay for at the club every Saturday.

When you begin to schedule your money, you will realize you really can go into **Department Store, Inc.** for toothpaste and walk out with nothing more!

When you begin to schedule your money, you will quickly learn how to do your own nails and feet until **Me, Inc.** can *afford* to put a cosmetologist on payroll.

When you begin to schedule your money, you will quickly learn how to detail your own car until **Me, Inc.** can *afford* the weekly detail at the carwash.

Get it? Even though you don't want to admit it, I know you do!

Scheduling your money is the easy part. You will simply look in **Bylaw Number Two** of the **"Check to Monday"** Workbook, and you will follow these rules:

1. Every time **Me, Inc.** receives money, **Me, Inc.** will distribute its money as follows:

   a. 10% – goes to **Me, Inc.** (savings account)

   b. 30% – gets put to the side, in cash, for whatever you will need (gas, bus fare, lunch money, etc.). I'll tell you later why it has to be in cash.

   c. 60% – goes into your checking account to pay **Everybody Else**.

2. If you tithe faithfully (and I strongly suggest that you do!), then you will follow these rules:

   a. 10% – goes towards tithes

   b. 10% – goes to **Me, Inc.** (savings account)

   c. 30% – gets put to the side, in cash, for whatever you will need (gas, bus fair, lunch money, etc.). I'll tell you later why it has to be in cash.

   d. 50% – goes into our checking account to pay
   Everybody Else.

3. **Me, Inc.** will not commit to pay anybody anything that
   can't fit into the schedule created as indicated above.

It's that simple.

Now, here's the hard part. You have a formidable opponent in the money game called **Haters, Inc.** **Haters, Inc.** wants **Me, Inc.** to lose. **Haters, Inc.** wants to win. Guess what? When **Haters, Inc.** wins, so does **Burger, Inc.**, **Department Store, Inc.**, and **Everybody Else.** The only loser is **Me, Inc.**

Haters, Inc. comes in many colors, shapes and sizes. Let me give you some examples.

Haters Inc. has a Spending Addiction

One of **Haters Inc.**'s best friends is **Spending Addiction**. **Spending Addiction** is what causes **Me, Inc.** to go to **Department Store, Inc.** for toothpaste and walk out with one hundred seventy-nine dollars and forty-seven cents worth of junk **Me, Inc.** doesn't even need, thus preventing **Me, Inc.** from properly scheduling its money.

You must show **Spending Addiction** who's boss! And I'm going to help you.

1. **Use cash for your incidentals**. Do not use a check card, a credit card, or even a personal check. Let me tell you why. If you go to **Grocery Store, Inc.** with the intention

of buying lettuce for the salad and you only take five dollars (cash) with you, you will not be tempted by **Spending Addiction**, who will definitely try to convince you to buy whatever is on sale with your personal check or debit/credit card. It's harder to spend more than you should when you are looking at the hard cash in your hand. Debit/credit cards and personal checks represent an endless supply of money that may not be available for **Me, Inc.** to spend. That's why you will use cash for incidentals, and personal checks for bills, until you break the CTM Syndrome.

Debit/credit cards are to be used in emergency situations and/or to reserve hotel rooms, airline tickets, etc.

2. **Stop window shopping.** **Spending Addiction** is lurking at every corner. What is window shopping anyway? Isn't that an oxymoron? If you don't have any money, stay home and spend some time with **Family, Inc.** Window shopping will remind you of all the money you don't even have to buy all of the stuff you probably don't even need. In fact, if you *are* window shopping, it probably *is* for stuff you *don't* need. I don't ever remember window shopping for toothpaste. I know you get the point.

3. **Stop hanging around People, Inc. who have a relationship with Spending Addiction.** Yes, I said it. Whoever **People, Inc.** happens to be — momma, daddy, sister, cousin, or friend. **People, Inc.** who try to "keep up with the Jones's" are even worse. Find **Other People, Inc.**, with different hobbies, to hang with. **People, Inc.**, who have relationships with **Spending Addiction**, will

tell you things like, "Girl, this new dress won't hurt, you owe it to yourself," and "Why are you working everyday if you can't afford to treat yourself to this $95 hairdo?" or "these $125 tennis shoes?" or "the latest $350 electronic device?" So, start hanging with **Other People, Inc.** who have other hobbies where **Spending Addiction** is afraid to lurk. Hobbies like investment clubs, book clubs, college courses, charitable organizations, and church (isn't it amazing that **Spending Addiction** goes cold turkey when its time to give back to the Lord?).

4. **Understand that Spending Addiction is just like every other addiction**. It amazes me how people who are robbing Peter to pay Paul look down on people who rob anybody to pay the drug dealer. It amazes me how people who went into the store for "just one thing" and came out with a cart full of stuff look down on people went to the riverboat for one quick game and didn't come out until 12 hours later – broke. It amazes me. I know it amazes you too. And I know you will end your relationship with **Spending Addiction** today.

Haters, Inc. likes Credit Cards Too

Haters, Inc.'s other close friend is **Credit Card**. In fact, **Spending Addiction** gave birth to **Credit Card**, making it possible for **Me, Inc.** to buy stuff **Me, Inc.** cannot afford. Stuff that **Me, Inc.** won't be able to afford for a long time. Stuff that initially costs $20, but winds up costing **Me, Inc.** $120 when **Interest, Inc.** comes to visit every month.

I know I don't have to tell you this, but I will mention it anyway. **Credit Card** makes it impossible for you to break the CTM Syndrome. **Credit Card** doesn't like you. In fact, **Credit Card** wants you to take as long as possible to pay off, because the longer you take, the more <u>**Me, Inc.**</u> loses, and the more **Credit Card**, **Spending Addiction**, **Haters, Inc.**, and **Everybody Else** win. I know I didn't have to tell you that part. I just threw it in anyway.

So, the next time an innocent cashier asks you to apply for a credit card so you can save 15% off of your next purchase, kindly respond, "No thank you. I would rather pay the 15% now than the 21% I will have to pay to **Credit Card** later."

Cashier, Inc. is definitely in cahoots with **Haters, Inc.**, **Spending Addiction**, **Credit Card**, and **Everybody Else**.

Beware!

Schedule Your Money Daily Principles

1. You must write down and know who **Everybody Else** is, so when it is time to pay, you won't be overbooked.

2. The first 10% of your money goes to **Me, Inc.**, the next 30% is set aside as cash for incidentals, and the remaining 60% is for **Everybody Else**. (Tithers: 10% tithing; 10% **Me, Inc.**; 30% incidentals; 50% **Everybody Else**).

3. **Haters, Inc.** will use **Spending Addiction**, **Credit Card**, and **Everybody Else** to keep you from winning the money game.

4. Cash is **Me, Inc.**'s only friend, and personal checks should only be used to pay regular bills, until you break the CTM Syndrome.

5. Stop window shopping. The end.

6. Stop trying to keep up with the Jones's. They're probably living from Check to Monday too.

7. Realize that spending money you don't have is an addiction and make sure you stick very close to this seven step program.

Bylaw Number Three:
Impregnate Your Dollars

*H*umans bear children who are an extension of both our wonderful qualities and our horrible flaws. That's how civilization continues. If you want your money to continue, then I suggest you apply the same principle – impregnate your dollars so they can have children who will have more children.

Now based on **Bylaws Number One** and **Two**, I know what you're thinking again (I read minds). *"Okay Miss Smarty Pants, so, I'm paying **Me, Inc.** first, and I've figured out how to pay **Everybody Else** second, and even though I'm no longer being catered to like the Queen of Egypt, I'm okay, but there is no **net profit** left to share with the investors. Hah! I am getting nowhere fast."* Right?

Umph, umph. You will soon learn not to test me. You are wrong again, my friend.

Remember when I said that consistency will one day put **Me, Inc.** in a position to duplicate itself? What I didn't tell you then is that when **Me, Inc.** gets paid, **Me, Inc.** puts its initial profit in a savings account at a bank on the other side of town so you, I mean **Me, Inc.**, cannot easily withdraw the money when times get a little tough. And you, I mean **Me, Inc.**, won't have a cash station card either.

The initial profit paid to **Me, Inc.** is going to earn interest and begin duplicating itself (having its own children) before **Me, Inc.** is even ready to duplicate itself. Therefore, when **Me, Inc.** needs a line of credit to buy a house or get a newer vehicle, then **Investors** will be willing to invest in **Me, Inc.** because **Me, Inc.** respected **Me, Inc** enough to pay **Me, Inc.** first, so the **Investors** can rest assured that **Me, Inc.** will do unto others as **Me, Inc.** has done unto itself.

It's the golden rule, dear. What you put out into the world comes right back to you.

Plus, there's a bonus. The money you paid to **Me, Inc.** begins to work for itself. Then the money has children that begin to work for themselves. That's called compound interest.

With no interest being earned, meaning you put the $100 monthly payment you make to **Me, Inc.** under a mattress instead of in a savings account, then in five years **Me, Inc.** will have $6000. Even at a meager interest rate of 5%, $100 per month in a savings account for 5 years yields $6828.94. Look at the chart below to see how these figures double and even triple over time.

	Mattress Money with No Interest	Savings Account at 5% interest	Mutual Fund / CD / or Savings at 9% interest
$100 per month for 5 years	6,000	6,828.94	7,598.98
$100 per month for 10 years	12,000	15,592.93	19,496.56
$100 per month for 20 years	24,000	41,274.63	67,289.60

Applying the same principle in **Bylaw Number 1**, if you now have an initial profit of $2000 per month, then **Me, Inc**., who always gets paid first, gets 10% or $200 each month. (**Everybody Else** has $1800 each month to do what they need to do — or $1600 for those who tithe — and that's more than enough money and if it isn't, then **Me, Inc.** needs to fire some **Employees** or cut some **Expenses**).

	Mattress Money with No Interest	**Savings Account at 5% interest**	**Mutual Fund / CD / or Savings at 9% interest**
$200 per month for 5 years	12,000	13.657.89	15,197.96
$200 per month for 10 years	24,000	31,185.86	38,993.12
$200 per month for 20 years	48,000	82,549.63	134,579.20

See, when you take one step towards anything good, five steps are taken towards you. When you consistently pay **Me, Inc.** first, a habit forms called money discipline. When you pick up the money discipline habit, you get other related habits by accident. You begin to watch where you spend your money and you begin to shop for sales and discounts. That's called being frugal. You've learned to work hard, so now you can play hard. Now that you have more discipline and you retain more of your initial profit, **Me, Inc.** has a good shot at permanently ending the CTM syndrome.

Impregnate Your Dollars Daily Principles

1. Your money must become pregnant if you want **Me, Inc.** to stay in business for future generations.

2. Save your 10% in a bank account on the other side of town, and decline the bank card so you cannot easily access this money when you are in trouble.

3. The 10% should be saved in an account that earns compound interest.

4. Money for vacations, new furniture, and other treats should be saved in a separate account and should come from the 30% set aside for incidentals and living expenses as indicated in **Bylaw Number Two: Schedule Your Money.**

5. The goal is to have at least six months of expenses saved before investing in more sophisticated financial tools.

6. Remember, what you put out into the world comes back to you.

Now, since we're talking about the golden rule . . .

Bylaw Number Four:
Treat Your Creditors As You Would Have Your Debtors Treat You

*T*his one is simple. It's "The Golden Money Rule" in action.

Remember when you loaned your cousin Pookie $50 you really didn't have and Pookie promised to pay you back as soon as he got paid? On payday, not only did you fail to see or hear from Pookie, but you heard from another cousin that Pookie was kickin' it at the club! You tried to call Pookie on the cell phone that your $50 helped to stay activated and now Pookie won't pick up your calls! Now, you *and* **Me, Inc**. are pissed!!

You want to do major bodily harm to Pookie.

You're calling everybody, telling anybody willing to listen, and of course, they all say, *"I would've told you not to loan Pookie your money in the first place. Didn't the same thing happen the LAST time you loaned Pookie some money?!?"*

And you say, *"You know, it's not the money, it's the principle. If Pookie didn't have the money, he could have just called me and said something."*

My point exactly.

Treat your creditors like you would want your debtors to treat you. When you signed on the dotted line at **Department Store, Inc.** for that new suit you just *had* to get for the wedding reception even though you have 50 other suits that you've only worn one time, then **Department Store, Inc.** expects payment when you promised to deliver it. When **Department Store, Inc.** cannot pay itself first because it loaned money to you that you won't or can't repay, then **Department Store, Inc.** is pissed.

And it hires pissed **Employees**, who no doubt suffer from the CTM Syndrome too, who call you and harass you for payment.

And when that doesn't work, they hire nice people who call you by first name when you answer the telephone!

But that's beside the point. The point is this — **Department Store, Inc.** can't pay **Everybody Else** because you won't pay them, and now **Department Store, Inc.** has to raise the interest rates for **Credit Card** in order to make the money you won't/can't/didn't pay!

See what you started?

Now some of us can't pay because we did not follow **Bylaw Number Two**, and since we have not scheduled our money, we have unfortunately double booked it and when the date arrives, either **Department Store, Inc.** or **Utility Company, Inc.** doesn't get paid and then **Credit Report** will pay the price for **Me, Inc.**'s shortcomings!

Sad, but true.

The rest of us have legitimate reasons for not being able to pay **Department Store, Inc.** on time. Maybe you got laid off. Maybe your car broke down and you needed to get it fixed and since **Bylaw Number One** hasn't been in place for long, you had to use your **Everybody Else** money to get the car fixed so you could get to **Job, Inc.** each day to even get the initial profit in the first place. I know. If it ain't one thing, it's another.

In either, case, you have a responsibility to call **Department Store, Inc.** to let them know what your situation is and when they can expect payment.

Just like Pookie had a responsibility to call you.

Since Pookie had to get such a small amount of money from you, I'm pretty sure Pookie didn't follow the rules of **Pookie, Inc.**, either. Pookie certainly ain't paying **Pookie, Inc.** first. And Pookie didn't schedule his money either. When Pookie borrowed that $50 from you that you really didn't have and Pookie promised to pay you back, Pookie probably forgot about all the other fifty dollars he promised to pay **Everbody Else** on the same day!!

Anyway, once you show **Department Store, Inc.** you are not playing them for a fool, you will find that **Department Store, Inc.** will probably do for you what you would have done for Pookie — give you the option to pay later or get on a more reasonable repayment plan until your situation becomes more promising.

Department Store, Inc. can relax now, because **Department Store, Inc.** knows when it will get payment from you, so now, **Department Store, Inc.** can schedule its money and duplicate itself!

Two more points:

1. If you loaned Pookie money that you didn't have, shame on you. If you can't afford to give it away, then don't loan it out in the first place. You never know who's *Living Check to Monday* these days!

2. If you have never loaned money *to* Pookie, then chances are you've probably *been* Pookie and instead of talking *to* you, I'm talking *about* you. In any case, follow **Bylaw Number Four** and the rest of us will pray for you.

Anyway.

Ten Commandments of the Golden Money Rule

1. Pay what you owe as you wish to receive what is due you.

2. Communicate with your creditors when you cannot pay.

3. The repayment amount for what you borrow must fit into your money schedule; if it doesn't fit, don't borrow it!

4. Do not lend to others what you cannot afford to give away.

5. Credit is a gift and should be treated as such.

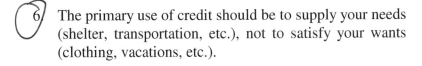

6. The primary use of credit should be to supply your needs (shelter, transportation, etc.), not to satisfy your wants (clothing, vacations, etc.).

7. With the exception of your primary automobile, do not use credit to acquire items that decrease in value.

8. Do not co-sign for others. If you must, make sure you are in control of making the monthly payment on time.

9. Check all three credit reports at least once per year: w w w . e x p e r i a n . c o m   w w w . e q u i f a x . c o m www.transunion.com. There are several online credit scoring and reporting services that will allow you to pull all three credit reports in one transaction.

10. Register for a credit monitoring service so you will be aware of important changes to your credit on a daily basis.

Buy Real Estate Instead of Deals at the Stake

I know what you're thinking. *"Just when this book was gettin' good, and I was feeling this whole **Me, Inc.** thing, this woman snapped. What in the world is a 'deal at the stake'?"*

Okay. I know I was stretching this one.

Let me tell you.

First, let's deal with the word "stake", then I can bring it on home for you. The word "stake" has many meanings. The meaning we'll deal with today is the one that, according to The American Heritage® Dictionary of the English Language: Fourth Edition, says, a "stake" is *"A vertical post to which an offender is bound for execution by burning."*

So, back in the day, if your butt was condemned to the stake, it literally meant your behind was going to burn to death. You were really through. Finished. Crispy. There would be nothing left of you but ashes.

My point exactly. Stop buying stuff that is no better than the ashes we can burn them to. Stuff that decreases in value the second you buy it. Stop making **deals at the stake**. Stop buying $100 gym shoes for teenagers who get D's in school. As a matter-of-fact, I don't care what kind of grades they get. Stop buying $75 jeans for kids who don't have $75 in the bank saved for their college education. Those shoes and jeans aren't worth the ashes you burn them to when they get raggedy 6 months later.

You thought I was going to stop with the **deals at the stake** you're making for the kids? Guess again. Now I'm driving in your lane.

Speaking of driving, stop buying the latest car that came out and pulling it up to your apartment. And if you buy a hoopty, stop buying rims that cost more than the car so somebody can take them.

Deals at the stake.

Stop buying every purse you see in the latest video. Clue, if the purse costs more than the amount of money you can keep in it on a regular basis . . . you know where I'm goin'. . .

Deals at the stake.

Stop spending $185 on your hair and nails and only $18.50 on groceries. Stop buying clothes to make you look good on the outside when what you really need is to make **Me, Inc**. feel good on the inside. **Deals at the stake**.

And Christmas. Oh, yeah. I got you know. Now the first thing I want you to know is that I love Jesus and I accept him as my Lord and Savior. I'm not gonna lie and tell you I tithe every single Sunday, but I am working on it. (Don't buy my pastor a copy of this book!!!)

But with all the love for the Lord we have, do you think He wanted us to spend our last dime and next month's rent showering each other with gifts that we could have bought for ourselves, or better yet, wouldn't dare think of using our own selves?!!?!! Do you think He wants us honoring Him by buying last minute bottles of ten-dollar-perfume because we found out Aunt So-'n-So was gonna be at Big Momma's house on Christmas and she probably got me something? Do you think your spoiled kids need another version of whatever the latest video game system is? I mean, how many different ways can we play Mrs. Pac Man?

Deals at the stake.

And on Christmas, too. You ought to be ashamed.

What happened to, *"It's the thought that counts?"*

Well, think about this.

Learn who the Lord truly is this Christmas. Discover the beauty of Kwanzaa this holiday season. Learn to love your neighbor as you would yourself. Stop cursing out the bill collectors you know good and well you owe. Read stories and sing some songs. I don't care what you do, but whatever you do, stop turning what is supposed to be the one time of year EVERYBODY gets some religion into ONE BIG **DEAL AT THE STAKE.**

Can I get an Amen?

Now, am I saying we all need to dress in rags and buy stock? No. I know you like to look good. I do, too. All I'm saying is, if you work hard, then you deserve to play hard. Make a conscious effort to avoid too many **deals at the stake**. If you don't, then the future of **Me, Inc**. is *at stake*. And the futures of **Son, Inc.** and **Daughter, Inc.** are too.

Spending Addiction, **Credit Card**, and **Hater's Inc**. are all closely related to **deals at the stake**. So, avoid **deals at the stake**. I know you're thinking, *"How do I do that?"* I told you, I read minds.

Here we go:

1.   Buy a used car. So you want a luxury car? Did you know that people who make over $100,000 a year often purchase pre-driven vehicles?   Now, I know we all need a car to get to **Job, Inc.**, but does it have to be fresh out of the factory? Did you know that if you buy the average car for $30,000 on Tuesday, that it's only worth $22,000 on Thursday if you try to sell it back? Now, if that ain't a **deal at the stake**, I don't know what is.

2.   Shop for clothing that can stand the test of time. I promise you those jeans that wrap around your thighs with a piece of cloth in between won't be cute in 6 months.

3.   Buy real estate. Real estate is the foundation for building family wealth and until you own where you live, most other investments just don't make good sense.

So, you've been renting for 10 years paying $900 a month. That's $10,800 dollars a year. $108,000 in ten years.

All that money for something that will never belong to you! All that money and what can you do with your rent receipts at the end of the year? Nothing.

You think you're afraid to pay a mortgage? Well guess what, you're paying someone else's mortgage, so why not pay your own! That's right. When you pay your rent, you are paying **Everybody Else's** mortgage. You and all of the other tenants. So, buy your family a house for Christmas and leave the latest video game system alone.

This is a bonus for those of you who've been shopping for *the perfect home* since the beginning of time and driving your real estate agent crazy – ***You should be ashamed of yourself!*** I mean, get real! You are not going to find your dream home on a **Check to Monday** budget and you probably will not get the same deal as the guy you saw on television at two o'clock in the morning. Your first home probably **will not** be your dream home . . . but then, neither is your apartment that you just paid one hundred eight thousand dollars for.

And another thing, stop shopping for mortgages like you shop for gas. The lowest payment may not always have the lowest interest rate and the lowest interest rate may not always be the best mortgage. Work with a licensed mortgage planner who will help you choose the best mortgage and payment for your individual financial goals and objectives. Am I telling you to be careless? Absolutely not. Just a friendly reminder that while you fight over 7% versus 7.125%, the interest rate on your rent is 900 Kazillion Percent!!!

So the moral of the story is this: buy real estate and leave the **deals at the stake** for the local fireman.

Buy Real Estate Daily Principles

1. Stop paying your landlord's mortgage. Immediately.

2. Unless you have a rich granddad, real estate is the beginning of your wealth building strategy.

3. Purchase a home that will fit into your money schedule, not what the lender says you can afford.

4. Chances are you will not get the same deal as the guy on television in the midnight hours, so stop driving your real estate agent crazy!

5. Interest rates are not like gas prices – you shouldn't simply drive down the street for the lowest one.

6. Your car note should be no more than one third of your mortgage payment.

7. Your first home is just the first step. Speak to a licensed mortgage professional who can help you develop an investment acquisition plan.

Me, Inc. Needs At Least 4 Siblings

*Y*es. **Me, Inc.** needs at least 4 brother and sisters.

Why?

Let me tell you.

Before I discovered that God was truly telling the truth when he condemned women to painful child labor, I wanted *five* kids. That's right. I wanted to have 5 kids out of my own body. You're probably thinking, why would a seemingly intelligent lady want *that many kids* in today's times? Well, one reason was I really wanted to bring people into the world and show them unconditional love. The biggest reason, though, is I wanted those 5 lives to show *me* some love when I get old. I figured it this way. When I get old, I don't want to be alone. It's really simple. I want a whole bunch of folk at my house every Sunday, just like Soulfood, cooking, cussing, crying, grandbabies crawling, whatever, just be at my house on a regular basis. So I figured if I had five kids, the probability of me being alone when I get old would be slim. So, if one kid got married and moved to another state, I would still have 4 more. If one joined the armed forces for life, I would have three to work with. If I just didn't like one for some reason, well you get the point.

Maybe you don't.

The whole point is this. What happens if you break your leg on the way home from the club and your disability doesn't kick in and you only have three sick days that you can get paid for at **Job, Inc.**? I'll tell you what happens. **Me, Inc.** is out of business! No more **deals at the stake**, and no *steak* either. Plus, the days of finding a job fresh out of school and working there for 50 years until you can retire and receive your pension are virtually gone!

That's why **Me, Inc.** needs at least 4 other **Siblings**, so let's call them "the crew" and you can name them **This, Inc.**, **That, Inc.**, **Us, Inc.**, and **They, Inc.**, so if one falls to the wayside, **Me, Inc.** can still eat!

That's called having multiple streams of income.

First off, if one of your multiple streams of income is from the sale of any type of illegal good or service, then I wish you luck until it runs out. You are what you eat and what goes around comes around. That's a fact. If your luck already ran out, or if you know people whose luck has run out – they're in jail, on drugs, or dead – then you know that nothing good will come out of anything bad. So let's eliminate the few dozen illegal things that can create income flow and focus on the millions of perfectly legal things that can do the same thing.

Now that we understand each other, we can move on.

So how is **Me, Inc.** supposed to use the **Siblings** to make some money?

Remember under **Bylaw Number One** I mentioned that every business provides goods or services in exchange for money? We dealt with the services that **Me, Inc.** provides in that section. In this section we are going to deal with the goods and services that can be provided by the **Siblings**.

As much as we complain about the price of food, do you really think you would want to eat burgers from **Burger, Inc.** if those burgers were free? Now, initially, you might say yes, but I beg to differ. If the burgers were free that would either mean the employees were not getting paid or the owner was doing all of the work himself. **Employees** who don't get paid, don't work. So your burger would be nonexistent or it wouldn't be quite as appealing to the taste buds. If the owner is doing all of the work himself, opening the store, mopping the floor, changing the garbage, preparing your burger . . . you get the point.

The moral of the story is this: stop providing your valuable goods and services for free! Have you ever wondered why people complain to you when you do the same thing for free that **Everybody Else** would have charged them for? I'll tell you why. **People, Inc.** don't appreciate free stuff! We don't apply value to anything until a dollar amount is attached to it. So take your family of gifts and talents and let's put the **Siblings** to work!

Get Paid for your Talents
Stop preparing your world class dressing every holiday and 1st Sunday for every neighbor and cousin who calls – for free. Charge $10 per pan and put **Dressing** and **Cake** on the **Family and Friends Stock Exchange**. Think about it. **Family** would rather pay $10 for your slap-the-judge-tasting dressing than have a mediocre pan for free.

The point is this: stop giving your talents away for free. Maybe you can at least make it from **Check to Wednesday** if you create another income stream with **Dressing, Inc., Pie, Inc., Car Wash, Inc.** and **Whateverothertalentsyouhave, Inc.**!

Use the Equity in Your Home to Finance Another Income Stream – Cautiously!

I know a ton of **People, Inc.** who have fifty, sixty, seventy thousand dollars or more of equity in their real estate – and they are *Living Check to Monday* with fifteen plus years left on the mortgage balance!

How ridiculous!

You have to use what you got to get where you want to be! Countless numbers of successful business people have leveraged the equity in their homes to build businesses, pay for education and training, or to otherwise enhance their lives and the lives of their families. So sit down, create a business/life plan and talk to a mortgage planner about using the equity in your home to get to the next level financially.

For the record: I am **NOT** in favor of using your home's equity to pay off **Credit Cards**, because most people charge the **Credit Cards** up again! What a waste. I do, however, encourage using the equity to finance a reasonable business venture that results in a steady stream of income that can pay off the credit card debt.

Get it?

I know you do . . .

But before you go, don't forget to incorporate **Me, Inc.** and the **Siblings**. No bootleg businesses here! Plus, you want to get the proper accounting and tax shields in place because Uncle Sam will surely come knocking on your door before **Everybody Else** gets a chance.

I'll tell you more about this in **Bylaw Number Seven**.

Me, Inc. Needs at Least 4 Siblings Daily Principles

1. Don't give your talents away for free.

2. Incorporate, incorporate, incorporate.

3. Create a life plan with 3-month, 6-month, 1-year, and 5-year goals.

4. Create a business plan for each of the **Siblings** with 3-month, 6-month, 1-year, and 5-year goals.

5. Consider using the equity in your home to finance one or more of the **Siblings.**

6. **DO NOT** use the equity in your home to pay off credit card debt.

7. Don't forget to incorporate **Me, Inc.** and all of the **Siblings**.

Master the Game with a Money Team

*I*f you play tomorrow's game by yesterday's rules, you will definitely lose. And if you don't have the expertise to know when the rules are changing, you may miss out on great opportunities to build, secure, and/or maintain your wealth.

So get yourself a money team:

1. Insurance Agent
2. Real Estate Broker
3. Licensed Mortgage Consulant
4. General Corporate / Real Estate Attorney
5. Accountant
6. Financial Planner
7. Estate Planning Attorney

Now, I know what you're thinking. *"Okay Miss Smarty Pants. I'm barely out of Spendaholics Rehab and here you go getting all technical on me like all of the other money experts. I knew it was too good to be true. I can barely afford to buy eyewater to cry with, so how do you expect me to afford to hire a money team???"*

Right?

Wrong!

Again!

Even the members of the 5-year-old little league have a full team and a coach to help them play the game. Why should you be any different?

It shouldn't cost you one penny to sit with an insurance agent to build an asset protection plan or a real estate broker to begin searching for your home or investment property. These are the first two members of your **Money Team**. You will, however, be required to pay a monthly insurance premium and of course, there are costs associated once you are ready to make an offer to purchase any piece of real estate.

You may have to spend anywhere from $50 to $300 to sit with a licensed mortgage consultant, depending on your needs. In most cases, getting pre-approved for a mortgage is free of charge, with the exception of credit fees. However, if you are trying to develop an investment acquisition plan, you may spend up to $300, depending upon the complexity of your needs.

The same goes for a financial planner. Consultation and plan development fees may range from $50 to several hundred, but again, the cost is minimal as it relates to the type and amount of wealth you are trying to build.

You have to spend money to make money!

Speaking of making money, you probably won't need an accountant until you've made enough money to count (and trust me, you would rather pay your accountant $500 - $700 out of your earnings to maximize your tax savings rather than pay Uncle Sam eight, nine, or ten times that amount in actual taxes!).

Furthermore, the corporate services/real estate attorney will typically charge somewhere between $500 and $1500 per corporate entity formed and somewhere between $250 and $500 per real estate closing (usually paid at the time of closing).

And finally, once you've got it all in place, money in the bank, insurance plans in place, a house for **Me, Inc.**, and **Siblings** making money, you will definitely need an estate planning attorney to help you decide who gets what when you pass on to **Heaven, Inc.**

You don't want **Family, Inc.** and **Perpetrators, Inc.** down here fighting over your **Stuff**. And yes, we all have **Stuff**. You don't want **Son, Inc.** or **Daughter, Inc.** giving the life insurance money to a con artist two weeks after your transition to "Check to Foreverland," if your intent was to allocate that money for college expenses and generational wealth. In fact, if you know your kids have problems that more than likely will not be solved in this millennium, then you may want portions of your estate to go to your children's children's children – and now, you're creating Generational Wealth (the Hiltons weren't made in a day!).

So after it's all said and done, an estate planning attorney, who will charge anywhere from $1,000 to $3,500, depending on your assets, is an important part of your team.

Just take it one team member at a time. And you, too, will have a **Money Team** that will coach you into living from *Check to Next Year*!

Master the Money Game with A Money Team Daily Principles

1. Secure one team member at a time.

2. Ask people you trust and trusted team members for related referrals.

3. Ask your team members for at least 5 referrals before commencing any business activities.

4. Check the 5 referrals!

5. Be honest with your teammates, no matter how embarrassing the situation.

6. Maintain open communication with your team members and don't hesitate to ask questions, questions, and more questions.

7. Tell other people about your team members and pass the wealth on to your friends and family!

Me, Inc. Resolutions

 hereas:

1. **Me, Inc.** will intentionally incorporate all of the Bylaws stated herein into **Me, Inc.**'s financial strategy;

2. **Me, Inc.** will be honest with thyself and will work daily towards purging all bad habits (Spending Addiction, Window Shopping, Keeping Up with the Jones's, etc.);

3. **Me, Inc.** will encourage **Others, Inc.** to purchase a copy of this book; and

4. **Me, Inc.** will work purposefully towards ending the **Check to Monday Syndrome.**

Be it resolved that Me, Inc. will be free from the CTM Syndrome by:

Month: _____
Year: _____
Signed: _____
        Me, Inc.

About the Author

K nown to thousands as the "Mortgage Guru," Lynn Richardson is much more than another mortgage and real estate professional helping families fulfill the American Dream. Author, broadcaster and motivational speaker, Lynn Richardson is a globally recognized wealth creation servant who not only wants to change the way Americans think about money, she wants to change how they treat it. With more than a decade of leading roles in the banking and real estate industries, Richardson's reputation as an authoritative, transformational financial educator resonates on a global scale, and has helped catapult thousands trapped in debt building habits into wealth creation lifestyles.

The Chicago native began her career in 1995 as a financial aid counselor at School of the Art Institute of Chicago, before landing a succession of leading roles in the mortgage industry. After joining American Home Mortgage in 1999, she was promoted to Assistant Vice President in 2003 and consistently ranked among the top one percent of more than 4,000 loan officers nationally. During her first five years in the mortgage lending industry, Richardson closed more than $100 million in mortgages across the nation. *One of her most notable cases is that of a lady who had four bankruptcies and two foreclosures, who became a successful homeowner after working with Richardson.* Richardson packaged her winning approach to helping consumers close on mortgage loans into the Mortgage Approval Plan, a signature industry tool used by top mortgage practitioners to assist consumers who need a roadmap to home ownership. Also, in 2003, Richardson created "*Wealth 'n Real Estate*," a flagship call-in talk show she continues to host for the nationally recognized Chicago station, WVON 1690 AM.

In 2006, Richardson joined JP Morgan Chase, and advanced to Vice President of National Strategic Partnerships, a coveted role responsible for creating mutually beneficial alliances with a multitude of entities and trade organizations. In 2006, Richardson was hand-picked to serve as the coordinator of The Delta Challenge Home Ownership Initiative, a signature economic development program of Delta Sigma Theta Sorority, Inc. In 2007, Richardson was responsible for implementing the Chase/AKA Keys to Homeownership Initiative, which leveraged the influence of the oldest black American sorority to further establish homeownership as the foundation for building wealth within the African American community.

In August 2008, Richardson was named National Home Ownership Advisory Council Chair of the Hip Hop Summit Action Network, a non-profit, non-partisan national coalition co-founded by entertainment and fashion mogul Russell Simmons and civil rights activist Dr. Benjamin Chavis that unites artists and executives, and advocates against poverty and injustice. In this capacity, she will serve as a fresh voice to the 59 billion dollar hip hop community promoting wealth creation through home ownership. During that same time, she launched the "*2008 HBCU Health, Wealth 'N Real Estate Tour*" as a result of her partnership with State Farm and the 50 Million Pound Challenge.

Richardson received a bachelor's of business administration in finance from Loyola University, IL, and is a licensed Real Estate Salesperson. Her memberships include Delta Sigma Theta Sorority, Inc., National Association of Real Estate Brokers, National Association for the Advancement of Colored People, Jack and Jill of America, Inc., and Rainbow Push Coalition. Her awards and recognitions are numerous, among them the 2007 Community Renewal Society 35 Under 35 Leadership Award. She and her best friend Demietrius have been married for 13 years. They have three daughters and call a South Chicago suburb home.

COMING SOON . . .Living Beyond Check To Monday:
A Spiritual Path to Wealth & Prosperity
By Lynn Richardson
Copyright © 2005 – 2008. All Rights Reserved.

It is easier for a camel to go through the eye of a needle, than for a
rich man to enter into the kingdom of God. Mark 10:25 (KJV)

So you mean to tell me that a big 900 pound camel has a better chance of squeezing through Madea's sewing needle than a rich man getting into heaven?

How many times have we said, when I start making more money, I'm going to help my church? Or even worse, when I get my money right, I'll start GOING to church? When I get on my feet, I'll start saving.   When the Lord blesses me with a new job, I'll start paying the bill collectors, even though I buy exotic coffee twice a day (reality check: any coffee that costs several dollars PER CUP is exotic in my book!).

When, when, when . . . sad to say, but every time we add a "when" clause, then we are demonstrating our trust in money and unfortunately, that means a whole lot of camels will be going through needles.

That also means we keep living from check to Monday.

You know, like I described in the other book. The CTM Syndrome: get paid on Friday, kick it on the weekends, pay "something on" the past due bills, and by Monday, we're broke! Then we pray, cry, worry, and do whatever it takes to get to the next payday and the cycle repeats itself.

So what do we do about it? What are you going to do about it? I think the scripture makes it plain and clear. We must replace our trust in riches with an unshakeable trust in God in order to achieve true wealth. But in order to trust something, we must understand it. So, like my first book, you bought this one out of desperation, borrowed it from a friend, or maybe you got it as a part of Bible study. The point is, you have it now. So pray for understanding, stay committed to a spiritual path to wealth and prosperity, and let's just hope and pray that we don't hear of any camels going through needles before we are transformed!

More Products by Lynn Richardson

Lynn Richardson's Wealth Building Kit
- Living Check to Monday
- Living Check to Monday Workbook
- Living Check to Monday Daily Tips CD
- Living Beyond Check to Monday
- Wealth 'n Real Estate CD Series
  o Buying Your First Home
  o Respecting Your Credit
  o Buying Investment Property
  o Creating Family Wealth
- Membership in Lynn's Wealth Building Club
- Bonus Books, Services and More!

Lynn Richardson's Debt Free Kit
- Living Check to Monday
- Living Check to Monday Workbook
- Living Check to Monday Daily Tips CD
- Membership in Lynn's Wealth Building Club

Lynn Richardson
. . .the mortgage guru

For More Information,
Contact Us:

Phone: 888.LYN.N123 (888.596.6123)

Email: dreamscometrue@lynnrichardson.com

Website: www.lynnrichardson.com